FORTRESS BOOKS

PRAYER

PRAYER

by

Olive Wyon

FORTRESS PRESS • PHILADELPHIA

Printed in U.S.A.   PO 6023   D63   UB2001

FOREWORD

The need for putting what we, as Christians, believe into words everybody can readily understand poses a constant challenge. In response to that challenge the New Testament itself was written in a language commonly spoken and understood. Through the ages handbooks, catechisms, and tracts have been written and, since the invention of printing, published to meet the need for clarifying in every age what it means to be a Christian.

Whether it is more difficult to be a Christian in one age than another is hard to say. But being a Christian in the second half of the twentieth century is becoming more and more complicated. This heightens the challenge of spelling out for our day in an uncomplicated way what it means to be a Christian. To put the thought patterns of theology into terms that are readily understood is not easy. Yet saying what we believe in such a way that others, without too much difficulty, will understand what we are talking about is the test of our own grasp of what we believe and hold to be true.

In tackling this task the authors of Fortress Books do not try to make a difficult faith seem easy but to make it easier for the reader to see how demanding Christian discipleship really is and how important it is for him to give meaning to what he believes in what he does. And so the authors want to give the reader clues to guide him in making his decisions from day to day. It is the hope of the publishers that these small books, dealing with central themes of Christian faith and life, may succeed in their purpose.

Helmut T. Lehmann
Editor

CONTENTS

THE SIGNIFICANCE OF PRAYER

"There is nothing more powerful than prayer, and there is nothing to be compared with it," says Chrysostom. If prayer is so important, then why is it so often neglected? the last thing we think of doing instead of the first? Millions of people ignore it completely; others question its importance: "After all," they say, "why should we pray? What is the point of it?" We could reply with a counter-question: "Why is it, then, that in some form or another prayer is practiced all over the world?" Simply regarded as a fact, it is no exaggeration to say that prayer is a universal human instinct. All over the world, at the present day, within every kind of religion, men pray.

For instance, in the icy wastes of the Arctic, a good friend of the Eskimos found as he lived among them and studied their customs and their ways of thinking that although their thoughts were often confused and bewildered by the mystery of the world in which they lived, yet they were deeply conscious of their weakness and limitation, and felt the need for help from mysterious higher powers. "In the face of the mysteries of life they had a sense of awe and the infinite." [1]

Their religion was animism of a primitive type. When these people heard of the love of God in Jesus their

---

[1] A. Lang Fleming, *Archibald the Arctic* (London: Hodder & Stoughton, 1957), p. 153.

hearts responded quickly and spontaneously. An Eskimo hunter said to the bishop one day, "Before you came the road was dark, and we were afraid. Now we are not afraid, for the darkness has gone away, and all is light as we walk the Jesus way." [2] These pagans had learned to pray, "Abba, Father." The change in them was so evident and so wonderful that those who had taught and served them in Christ's name were amazed and awed as they listened to these men and women praying so trustfully and truly, thanking God for their deliverance from all their fears. Theirs was indeed a "new creation."

In the world of Islam, with its millions of convinced followers, prayer takes a central place. In the whole Moslem world it is laid down that every Moslem must pray five times a day: at daybreak, at noon, in the afternoon, at sunset, and at night. Never can I forget the experience of standing by the open window, on a spring evening at sunset, in the old city of Istanbul, and hearing from a minaret close at hand the muezzin chanting the Call to Prayer: "God is most great. . . . I testify that there is no God but Allah. . . . I testify that Mohammed is Allah's apostle. . . . Come to prayer. . . . Come to security. . . . God is most great. . . . There is no God but Allah." From the heights of Scutari I was wakened about two o'clock in the morning by the distant Call to Prayer from a mosque across the water, with the added words, "Prayer is better than sleep." Lyman MacCallum, a great friend of the Turkish people, would often slip into a mosque for the sunset prayer. He was deeply impressed by the reality and seriousness of this act of worship. He had many Moslem friends, and they would tell him how

---

[2] *Ibid.*, p. 183.

often in this common prayer in the mosque they would forget that there were hundreds of other people there, because they were so lost in the sense of awe at the greatness of God.

Lilias Trotter, another missionary in the Moslem world, gives her impression of a congregation at prayer in a mosque in Algeria: "I wish I could give the feeling of it, the great dim mosque lit by rows of tiny lamps, open on all sides to a court in brilliant starlight, with trees and a splashing fountain. Then the rows of solemn white figures, rising and falling simultaneously in their prostrations like the waves of the sea. . . . After a pause of silence there began a kind of wail, 'Allah! Allah! Allah!' There was an indescribable moan in the intonation, a crying out for the living God." [3]

There is a great deal of prayer in the Buddhist world. In Tibet, it has been said, possibly prayer is more widely practiced than in any other country in the world. We have all heard about their prayer flags and prayer wheels, and we may be tempted to dismiss these practices as "rank superstition," but the few Europeans who have penetrated below the surface believe that behind the outward ceremonies and popular practices there is a great deal of genuine longing for God. Now and then Buddhists in various lands come in touch with Christian people, and in friendly intercourse it becomes evident that these men have already a certain experience of prayer, and a great desire for further light on the mystery of life.

A moving modern instance comes from Formosa. In

---

[3] C. E. Padwick (ed.), *The Master of the Impossible* (London: Society for Promoting Christian Knowledge, 1938), p. 52.

1895 a boy, Tao-Ying, was born into a very religious Buddhist family, whose forebears had come to the island from South China. From his earliest years there was "something different" about this boy. He was lovable and attractive and very thoughtful, with a great love of solitude and of the beauty of nature. At the age of sixteen he entered a Buddhist monastery as a novice. His head was shaved and he was given a new name: Tao-Ying (Hero of Truth) was now called Miao-Chi (Mysterious Joy). The new novice took his first year in the monastery very seriously. He became rigorously disciplined, especially in speech, and his fellow-novices were astonished at the way in which in the midst of a busy day he would always spend a good deal of time in meditation. He was an apt pupil, with marked intellectual gifts, which were developed by years of study and meditation, at first in Formosa and later in Japan and in China.

One day, while Miao-Chi was staying in a monastery of the Zen Buddhist school, in Japan, on May 25, 1920, he had a memorable experience. He was sitting in the Hall of Meditation, thinking, reading, and praying. Through the open windows the songs of the birds and the fragrance of the lilies drifted in from the garden. In the pamphlet he was reading, the writer quoted the words, "For God hath placed eternity in their hearts." These words impressed him profoundly. Hour after hour he sat on, lost in thought. As he meditated upon them he began to see that for those who "carried eternity in their hearts" all human barriers were down. No longer would there be divisions between friends and enemies, foreigners and fellow countrymen, but all men everywhere would be of one family. This impression was so overwhelming that it was far into the night before he returned to his cell to sleep. From that day the monks noticed a great difference in him, but no one dared ask him any questions. In East Asia in such matters reticence is the rule. This experience was the beginning of his conversion.

Through his studies in comparative religion, and in various personal contacts, Miao-Chi began to feel greatly attracted to the great *bodhisattva* of the West, Jesus Christ, who was the inspiration of many great men and women about whom he had read. In his talks and lectures he would often speak of Christ among other great men. Already this young monk was a valued teacher and spiritual guide. But, as years went on, his own soul was desperately thirsty. On the night of March 5, 1928, he prayed, almost in despair, "O Heaven! have mercy upon me, send me a teacher who can lead me to the light!" The next morning a Swedish missionary who was visiting Formosa and had heard about this wonderful young abbot, called upon him at the monastery. This visit of Dr. Reichelt led to a deep friendship between the two men. Step by step Dr. Reichelt answered the abbot's questions and led him on into the heart of the Christian faith. They often prayed together. One day, after much prayer and discussion, the young abbot turned to his friend saying very quietly and solemnly, "At this moment, in the presence of God, I solemnly vow to devote my life to Christ." A few days later, after an unforgettable time of prayer and dedication, the two friends parted. After this Miao-Chi passed through a time of great difficulty, and suffered persecution and imprisonment. Two years later, he died in a Christian hospital, having borne a noble witness to Christ the only Savior.[4]

These modern instances of the worldwide instinct for prayer could be multiplied a thousandfold. This raises a further question: Why do men pray?

Some words of St. Paul during his visit to Athens give us the answer. He had been walking through the city, looking with distaste at the objects of worship on every hand, but at one point he had noticed a simple altar with a strange inscription, "To an unknown god." He turned to his cultured, critical audience and said plainly, "What therefore you worship as unknown, this I proclaim to you." He then began to proclaim the greatness of "God who made the world and everything in it, being Lord of heaven and earth. . . . And he made from one every nation of men to live on all the face of the earth," Paul said, "that they should seek God, in the hope that they might feel after him and find him. Yet he is not far from each one of us, for 'In him we live and move and have our being.'"

In other words, St. Paul is suggesting that we pray, or we want to pray, because *God is;* he is the Living God, who has made us for himself. Paul had no time to develop this point any further, it is true, for his audience was both critical and impatient. Probably he would have gone on to say more about God, the only true God, as the Creator, and he would have explained that this does not mean that God made the world once for all and then left it to its own devices. Rather, he would have spoken of "continual creation" in the language of Psalm 139:

---

[4] K. Reichelt, *The Transformed Abbot,* pp. 132-34.

Thou searchest me, Eternal One, thou knowest me,
  thou knowest me sitting or rising,
  my very thoughts thou readest from afar. . . .
Thou art on every side, behind me and before,
  laying thy hand on me.
Such knowledge is too wonderful for me;
  it is far, far beyond me.   (Moffatt)

That is, long before we knew anything about it, God made us out of nothing, brought us into being, fashioned us according to his purpose, and made us able to do his will. When this great reality dawns upon us we realize that there can be no neutrality in our attitude toward God; the fact that he, in love, has made us for himself is a call to decision. We must be for him or against him. We must either turn away from him in rebellion, or we must give ourselves to him in worship. Henceforth our attitude toward him is one of obedience and trust.

Then we find that the meaning of the universe has been disclosed: the will of the great and glorious Creator should be fulfilled in the life of each of us. This, we see, is not a hard, impossible, abnormal ideal. It is the fact, borne out by experience, that God's will is literally the very best thing for us all. As the key fits the lock, as the bird flies in the air, as the fish swims in the water, so each of us is "in our element" when we live in God, and want only to do his will. Then we can fly, or walk, or stand still, as he wills. For we know that whether hard or easy this is the right way, and the only way, because he alone is our All, our Father and our Friend.

To enter the world of prayer, therefore, is to enter a

new world. Everything it touches is transformed, from the life of the individual and the human family to the furthest borders of man's history and beyond. "Behold," says our Lord, "I make all things new."

THE ORIGIN OF PRAYER

Prayer begins with *God,* and not with ourselves. This is the fact of fundamental importance when we are thinking about prayer. A great deal of talk about prayer, and a good deal of writing about it is beside the mark because it ignores this fact. Unfortunately, in our self-conscious, man-centered age, it is only too easy to be interested in prayer, to be ready to discuss it at length in a study group, to read books about it, and to get no further. Any spark of genuine desire for it is then stifled in the barren atmosphere engendered by endless discussion and fruitless reading. This frivolous attitude toward prayer—as though it were an interesting psychological experience—prevents us from learning to pray. Even when we are in earnest about it, we often make no progress because we are too engrossed in ourselves, too anxious to watch our reactions, too ignorant of the true meaning of prayer. It is fatally easy to be regarded as a "very religious" person, and yet to be so absorbed in what *we* think, what *we* believe, what *we* want to know and to feel, that we cannot even see the object of prayer. We have not begun to see that all that matters is that God should be at the very center of our lives, and that his will should be done, and done as far as possible through us.

Think of the world in which we live. There are people who have never heard of the true God, or of Jesus Christ our Savior; yet, as we have already seen, they are feeling after him by prayer and sacrifice. To many others, God is merely a name, totally irrelevant to this "modern age." Some deny his existence altogether. Where the Christian church has been planted for centuries there are a great many people who would say that they believe in God, but by their lives it is evident that they hardly ever think of him, to them he is remote and unreal. All they want is comfort and security. Sin, suffering, and death are outside their reckoning. It is only when they are plunged into trouble of some kind that they may begin to feel God nearer than they expected, and then perhaps they may begin to try to pray.

But what about we who call ourselves Christians, we who are members of the church of Christ, and do many "good works"? What is our attitude? We know what it ought to be—for us God is All. He means everything; without him we are lost in a universe without a solution. The whole universe is gathered up into him, and in him all things cohere. He is before all things—before we were aware of him, before we had any being, he created us and redeemed us. "While we were yet sinners Christ died for us." So we already belong to him by his own act and choice. He has claimed us for himself. He has laid his hand upon us. Each of us can say, with wonder and adoration, "I come from God, I belong to God, I go unto God."

Yet although we may admit that this view is a fundamental truth, in actual practice we often forget it. We live as though everything depended upon ourselves, even though we may call God in now and then, to try to get us out of our confusion. We tend to put "doing" before "being." We live in a hustle and are brimming over with zeal and good works. Too often we suffer from the delusion that we can do a great deal off our own bat. We have forgotten that what we do is not nearly so important as the way in which we do it; in the last resort this depends upon the kind of people we are. For the only life that can be fruitful is one in which all we do is "begun, continued, and ended in God."

There may be times when we are even tempted to say to ourselves, "But since God is so good, and he has given us this work to do, why do we need to pray? Why should we pray?" This is a specious argument. It sounds more convincing than it is. The only convincing answer is the fact that Jesus prayed. If he prayed, and put it before everything else, how much more do we—sinful, ignorant people—need to pray. Here we are faced by a great mystery. The fact that our Lord prayed as man is bound up with the mystery of his Person, as true God and true man. The only clue for our own lives comes from the evidence of the Gospels which show us that Jesus lived in daily and hourly dependence upon God: "The Son can do nothing of his own accord, but only what he sees the Father doing. . . . I can do nothing on my own authority. . . . My Father is working still, and I am working." As we read the Gospel story we notice how often it is said that Jesus "looked up" in the trustful, loving expression of his dependence upon the Father. It is obvious that the whole of life did not lie open before him like a map, with the way he should go marked clearly upon it. He had to make his decisions and do his works in a responsible human manner, yet all were made in complete surrender to the will and the power of God his Father.

This is not easy for us to understand. In fact we can only begin to understand it in the light of the "paradox of grace" and the "paradox of the Incarnation." [1] The Jesus of the Gospels was steeped in the consciousness of God: "The man in whom God was incarnate would claim nothing for himself as a man, but ascribed all glory to God." [2] This is very mysterious, but it throws a flood of light on the meaning of prayer. Jesus is the master of prayer. If we want to learn to pray, one of the first things he shows us and tells us is this: all comes from God, of ourselves we can do nothing.

The Gospel story shows us that Jesus lived a real life upon this earth. He was not a god masquerading as a man. We know that Jesus was born into a God-fearing, deeply religious home-circle, which belonged to the "quiet in the land." We know that he spent the greater part of his life at Nazareth, but we know nothing about it. We can only infer, from the power and confidence with which he came forth to preach and teach and heal, that all through those years he had been growing in love and wisdom and had become ever more deeply aware of his dependence upon his heavenly Father, till he could say that it was his meat and his drink to do his will. Not that he had ever been disobedient or had ever wanted to set his will against the will of the Father, but rather that through prayer and obedience and love he had en-

---

[1] Donald M. Baillie, *God Was in Christ* (London: Faber and Faber, 1948), pp. 106ff.

[2] *Ibid.*, p. 126.

tered so deeply into the Father's purpose for the world that his whole being was set on following the path which finally brought him to the cross. During the years of his public ministry we read of frequent withdrawals into the quiet of the desert or the hills, or of trips across the lake from the busy shores of Capernaum and other towns to the quiet of "the other side." All through the last week of his life he sought solitude for prayer on the Mount of Olives. It was in his place of prayer that he was arrested. He died praying, with the words of a psalm upon his lips.

To know that prayer begins with God, and not with ourselves, that he loves us and wants us, that even the faintest desire to pray has been kindled in our hearts by his Holy Spirit, releases us from tension. "Come," he says, "for all things are now ready." The way is open—at great cost—for "God was in Christ reconciling the world to himself."

So we turn to prayer quietly, confidently, as God's beloved, forgiven children, and we use the tender word that Jesus gave us, saying, "Abba, Father." Our prayer will be transformed if we always take time for a moment or two of preparation—if we reflect on the greatness and the mercy and the nearness of the God to whom we are coming. Instead of plunging immediately into distracted petitions about our own affairs (which only increases our confusion of mind), we shall begin by waiting upon God in quiet faith. Our prayer will be more real, and far more effective, if we remember to make brief pause for preparation, if for a few moments we stop talking, and try to hold ourselves still before God. As we wait we can make brief acts of faith such as, "God is here, and God is love. . . . Christ is here with me at this moment. . . . He will never let me go. . . . He says *fear not.*" Simple affirmations of this kind enable us to put ourselves and our needs into God's hands, and to see first of all that he may be glorified. Once we have entered into this rest, which may coincide with a normal active life, our hearts will be strangely lightened, we shall find that we are less self-concerned, less troubled by the sight of our sins and miseries, for we are now more willing to face the truth about ourselves. Then we can rejoice in God, in his love and beauty, his power and his grace, knowing that his love is constantly being poured out upon us, and upon all the world.

A young man of the present day found this rest in the midst of the torture of continual interrogations and brainwashing in Chinese prisons. When he was near the end of his imprisonment (although he did not know it), when he feared the "spectre of madness," due to the ceaseless assaults upon his mind and his will—then, as he says, "in the quietness of my last cell . . . all I could cry out in my anguish was 'I believe. I believe.' It was the last stand . . . the only thing that was going through to the end." [3]

Such faith, and such power to endure, is not won in a day. It is given and maintained by the grace of God to those who are singlehearted in the day of obedience, even in the smallest things and in the most ordinary and prosaic conditions. Objectivity of this kind implies a life

---

[3] Geoffrey T. Bull, *God Holds the Key* (London: Hodder & Stoughton, 1959), p. 158.

of quiet and humble dependence upon God—for everything. In practice this means the willing acceptance of difficult or uncongenial conditions of life and service, the acceptance of trials and temptations, from both without and within, of all kinds. It means being willing to "be" what we are—weak, tempted, often afraid, empty of all good. This is the death of self. Further, it means being willing to go anywhere, to do anything, or to give up anything that God may call us to do or to renounce. In short, it means being at God's disposal, "ready for his perfect will."

PRAYER AS RESPONSE

Christian prayer is the highest kind of prayer. It is man's response to God's revelation of himself. This revelation includes the whole vision of God which the Bible contains, experiences of prophets and psalmists as well as the supreme revelation of God in Christ in the New Testament. "The nature of God is the key to prayer." In other words, all our attempts at prayer are our efforts to respond—however imperfectly—to the God who is so gracious that he calls us to worship him. The words of Jesus about the kind of worshipers God desires are very gracious and gentle, and yet deeply demanding as well: "God is spirit, and those who worship him must worship in spirit and truth. . . ." In all true prayer, revelation becomes personal. We now know, "This means me!" And when we come to realize this truth it matters supremely, not only for us, but for the whole world.

This response involves a great deal more than we realize. If we think religion is easy, and that we ought to be able to pray "straight off," as some people think, if we depend wholly upon our own efforts, and do not even ask to be taught because we think we have nothing to learn, then we shall not get very far. Our religion will remain a very limited, shallow affair, and our prayers will be equally limited, and sometimes childish. Some people never grow up in their prayer life. The prayers they used at sixteen, they still use at sixty. There may be various reasons for this arrested development. It is not always the fault of the person concerned. It may be the fault of the church to which he or she belongs. These people have not gone forward because no one has shown them the way, indeed, they are not aware that there is a way. Others "stick" in the way of prayer because they have wrong, hard, unbelieving thoughts of God, others because they do not think about him enough to want him, they do not feed on the Word of God. Perhaps they are content with snippets from the Bible or from other religious books, to give them a fillip now and again. Or perhaps they fall back on a few familiar prayers, either of their own making, or from a book which may have helped them several years before. They have no idea that beyond them lies a world of prayer, which leads on to the very limits of this earthly life and, indeed, is the only life which goes on, over the river of death, into the unseen world beyond.

So when we begin to want to pray, or to pray better, the first thing we must do is to think. The prophet Isaiah brings this out vividly in his picture of a great assize. Here God convicts his people of their sin, the sin of forgetting and forsaking him, their God, to whom they owe everything. Yet they think they are "very religious." They offer prayers and sacrifices, they crowd the courts of the temple and offer their worship with zest and zeal. But God says, "You do not think." Before we can have any true religion, or offer any acceptable sacrifice, we need to be awake to listen to the voice of God to show us our sins and to lead us into true repentance. Writing

on this passage, George Adam Smith points out that
God's people were guilty of the three besetting sins of
religious people: "Callousness in worship, carelessness in
life, and the temper which employs the forms of religion
simply for self-indulgence or self-aggrandisement." [1]
Through the burning words of the prophet "God compels
them to think." He asks them: "What do I care how you
multiply those victims of yours? I have had enough and
to spare. . . . Think you it is a welcome sound, the tramp
of your feet in my courts, bringing worship such as
yours? Vain offerings, bring them no more. . . . Hold out
your hands as you will, you shall get no heed from me;
add prayer to prayer, I will not listen; are not those
hands stained with blood?" (Isa. 1:12-15, Knox)

These terrible words were intended to awaken the
consciences of these careless worshipers whose religion
was so shallow and so unreal that it had no connection
with real life. They were offering prayers and sacrifices,
but at the same time they were oppressing the poor.
They ignored the social wrongs at their very doors, and
even participated in these abuses themselves. In every
country and in every generation we need to listen to
this word of God.

The Abbé Pierre, who has done so much to stir people's consciences on behalf of the homeless people in
Paris, as well as in many other ways, has scathing
words to say to us today: " 'I'm hungry! I'm deserted!
I'm in pain. . . . I'm in pain,' says God through a million,
million human voices down the centuries. And in them
speaks the judgment, a living judgment, a whirlwind

---

[1] George Adam Smith, *Book of Isaiah* (5th ed.; London: Hodder
& Stoughton, 1890), I, 6.

that is bearing down upon us, or that we are drawing down by our own actions, a whirlwind of happiness or of frenzy." [2] And so he challenges us *to think.*

If in his earlier years Isaiah had ever been guilty of sharing in the too-easy outlook of the public religion of his own day, a great experience which he describes later on changed him completely. "In the year that King Uzziah died"—this is not so much a historic date as a recollection of a great experience. Uzziah had been guilty of presumption and—so it seems—had then flown into such a passion of rage that a latent disease broke out all over his body. From that moment he dwelt alone, cut off from his people. And now he had died, and Isaiah went into the temple to pray. And as he prayed he had a great vision: "I saw the Lord sitting upon a throne, high and lifted up. . . ." The vision of the majesty and the holiness of God dawned upon the young prophet; the walls of the earthly temple fell away, and in spirit he was in the wide spaces of the unseen world, listening to the songs of adoration of the heavenly choirs chanting antiphonally, "Holy, holy, holy, is the Lord of hosts." And as Isaiah watched and listened he saw a thick mist rising from the ground, a mist caused by the meeting of holiness and sin. And he "felt the shame, the distraction, the embarrassment of a personal encounter with One whom he was utterly unfit to meet." [3] He was overwhelmed by the presence of the Holy God. In that

[2] Abbé Pierre, *Man Is Your Brother* (London: Geoffrey Chapman, 1958), p. 5.

[3] Smith, *op. cit.*, p. 69.

19

presence he saw himself as he really was—in God's sight. "Woe is me!" he cried out in anguish. "For I am lost; for I am a man of unclean lips, and I dwell in the midst of a people of unclean lips; for my eyes have seen the King, the Lord of hosts!" And immediately, at the very moment that he confessed and disowned his sin and the sin of his people, mercy came to him: "Then flew one of the seraphim to me, having in his hand a burning coal which he had taken with tongs from the altar. And he touched my mouth, and said: 'Behold, this has touched your lips; your guilt is taken away, and your sin forgiven.' "

This wonderful vision brings out the close connection between adoration and confession. Adoration comes first, for we cannot see ourselves truly save in the sight of God and his holiness. Above all, it is at the cross that we see what sin means. The men who put Jesus to death were not bandits or criminals, they were respectable, educated, official people. But self-interest, personal ambition, dislike of change, moral cowardice, and self-will crucified the Lord of Love. "All who seek their own will are of the company of his crucifiers," says William Law. In that light we all stand condemned. For penitence is not an expression of disappointment with ourselves, that is merely vanity. We come to true repentance when we see that sin is so terrible because it is an offense against the love and the majesty of God. That is why Isaiah exclaimed, "I am lost!" He knew that he could never make up for what he had done wrong. Nor can we, and we are always in debt to God until we ask to be forgiven and he blots out our sin and gives us his peace.

Repentance begins with seeing that we have sinned. Until that light shines into our minds we may easily deceive ourselves, thinking of our faults as "little sins," or perhaps only as "weaknesses," or as simply due to "our temperament." When we do begin to see, our first reaction—like that of the prophet—is one of horror and shame. Then we begin to realize what an injury we have done to God as well as to man. True and honest confession, with any possible restitution we can make, is the most that we can do. But we must bear the consequences of our sin, without indulging in futile remorse. By every means in our power we must believe and accept the forgiveness of God; we must go regularly to Holy Communion, and live as God's forgiven children. Confession is an integral element in prayer, not only when we have passed through some intense experience. Much staleness of spirit, listlessness in good habits, and aloofness, both from God and man, may be caused by sins unconfessed and ignored which have built up a wall of separation cutting us off from real communion with God and man. So whether we are aware of sin or not, we all need to pray constantly for the grace of true repentance, using the words of Psalm 51: "Create in me a clean heart, O God, and renew a right spirit within me."

The response of adoration and confession issues directly in the response of dedication. The moment that the prophet knew that his sin had been taken away, he was able to hear the voice of God addressed to himself: "And now I heard the Lord say, Who shall be my messenger? . . . . and I said, I am here . . . make me thy messenger" (Knox), or, in the version with which we are familiar, "Here am I; send me." His response is free and spontaneous. For now his will is one with God's will, and all he wants is to please and serve him wherever and in whatever way he may choose.

This response is all-important. In the last resort the life of the church as a whole depends upon the response of each individual Christian to the call of God. Each life of prayer, however hidden and unknown, is a small but integral part of the life of the whole church. Church history shows that when the personal life of worship and prayer begins to flicker and die out, the life of the church as a whole declines. As Evelyn Underhill points out, "Revival has always come through persons for whom adoring and realistic attention to God, and total self-giving to God's purpose, have been the first interest of life. These persons, it is true, have become fully effective only when associated in groups; but the ultimate source of power has been the dedication of the individual heart." [4]

This dedication of the will is not easy. It asks from us a persistent, gradual, patient, and ever-deepening surrender to God's call at every point in our lives. Bit by bit, here a little and there a little, body, mind, and spirit are offered to God.

This response of the will is expressed both in secret prayer and in outward action. The unification of life which this requires is attained chiefly by what is often called the "sacrament of the present moment." This is

---

[4] Evelyn Underhill, *Worship* (London: James Nisbet, 1936), p. 166.

the state of mind which sees God always at work, always present, loving, and giving. Every moment of our lives we discover him at work in the life around us as well as in our own lives. For every duty, every pleasure, every call to self-sacrifice or to suffering, is to be accepted from his hands, and woven into the fabric of our lives. People sometimes say that they have no time to pray. But a person whose one aim in life is to do the will of God *is* praying at every moment, whether by acceptance of the duty and claim of the moment or by a momentary act of loving worship to the God who is ever pouring out his love and his grace upon us.

THE PRACTICE OF PRAYER

Prayer is of two kinds—the state of prayer and the act of prayer. In this chapter we are thinking of the act of prayer, as a specific activity which gives meaning and power to the rest of life.

The practice of prayer consists in a balanced use of discipline and freedom. Discipline comes first, however, for we can never learn anything without going through a period of effort which may sometimes amount to a test of endurance. The accomplished musician has years of hard work and unceasing practice behind him before he appears on the concert platform. The apparent ease and mastery of his art is due to the cultivation of a gift which might otherwise have never come to fruition. Prayer is our response to the love of God, it is true, but our previous history is a great handicap. Since we are not accustomed to putting God first, almost unconsciously we still want to go our own way, even in prayer. We resent the very idea that we may have to use some force to keep ourselves up to the resolution we have made in an hour of vision and dedication. Our dedication has to be worked out in actual life, and that is where the "inherited spirit of revolt," the ingrained habit of self-will, makes it difficult to follow the new path of prayer and humble obedience.

So we must accept the fact that a disciplined life of prayer will cost us a great deal. Christian life is often spoken of as a warfare. This applies not only to outward difficulties, but still more to the struggle against our own slackness, our inconstant will, our fluctuating desires, as well as against sin in all its forms. We must be prepared to have a hard time of it, for months or even for years. But if we are faithful and hold firmly to our initial dedication to God and his will, in the end we shall come out into a "large place"; and as we look back we shall see that every step of the way has been necessary.

This discipline affects every part of our life, inward and outward. Since we are "body-soul" beings, we need to take into account such matters as the control of our habits of sleeping, eating, and drinking, exercise and recreation, as well as our hours of work. What most of us need is not asceticism, but moderation or balance. Common sense tells us that over-indulgence in food or drink or pleasure or recreation will play havoc with our prayers just as much as an excess of rigid self-denial.

The body is the temple of the Holy Spirit, and it is obvious that if this temple is to be kept clean and bright and quiet for the Lord, we need to be wise and sensible about everything that affects our health and efficiency, so far as this lies in our own power.

The same truth applies to the mind, the control of the mind by habits of concentration, the wise use of relaxation, the alternation of intellectual and manual occupations, and the like. Everyone who tries to pray is beset with wandering thoughts. Some of this is inevitable and is best ignored, but there may be a good deal of indulgence in daydreaming and foolish fantasies, which does not stop of itself because we are now trying to pray. Control of all our thoughts will help us to be more controlled in our minds when we turn to prayer. St. Paul speaks of "bringing every thought into captivity to the obedience of Christ." It is obvious that the habit of brooding, the secret dwelling on harsh, resentful, or self-pitying thoughts, is the opposite of "obedience to Christ." Such thoughts are like festering sores in our minds, influencing our words and our behavior, whether we are aware of this or not.

This emphasis upon the need to discipline our thoughts is closely connected with another element which is often overlooked—the Bible lays great stress upon the discipline of speech. Jesus speaks very strongly about this: "I tell you, on the day of judgment men will render account for every careless word they utter; for by your words you will be justified, and by your words you will be condemned." St. James too urges the need for control of the tongue in language that is so fierce that it suggests an intimate knowledge of the harm done by unkind, malicious, thoughtless words: "We all make mistakes in all kinds of ways, but the man who can claim that he never says the wrong thing can consider himself perfect, for if he can control his tongue he can control every other part of his personality! . . . . The human tongue is physically small, but what tremendous effects it can boast of! A whole forest can be set ablaze by a tiny spark of fire, and the tongue is as dangerous as any fire, with vast potentialities for evil. It can poison the whole body; it can make the whole of life a blazing hell" (Phillips).

We need to pray constantly, especially before any

social occasion, "Cleanse the thoughts of my heart by the power of thy Holy Spirit," and, "Set a guard over my mouth, O Lord, keep watch over the door of my lips!" [1]

Self-discipline leads into a far greater freedom than we have ever known before. Far from feeling bound we feel free. The fact that we are giving ourselves more and more fully to God sets us free from all kinds of hindrances: from our moods, whims, and fancies; from self-centered desires; from letting good impulses peter out into nothing, as well as from inordinate desires or obsessions, which make us feverish in the effort to satisfy them. When we failed to satisfy them, we felt frustrated, but if we succeeded, we found that everything we touched turned to dust and ashes. On the other hand, in a disciplined life, with prayer at the center, we find that our morbid scruples and our fear of offending God have disappeared. We are now sure that God is love, that we and all his children are in his keeping, that though we are aware of our weakness and sinfulness, we are still at rest in God's mercy. We begin to know something of the joy of life because we are running in the way of God's commandments. For "his service is perfect freedom."

There is a close connection between this emphasis upon discipline and freedom, and the question of method in prayer. The necessity for method is based on the obvious fact that whatever we do repeatedly and punctually tends to become second nature. For instance,

---

[1] Psalm 141:3.

when we begin to learn to ride a bicycle how awkward we feel, what attention we have to give to every movement and how we wobble about! Yet in a very short time we can mount the cycle and ride off, almost without thinking about it. Our movements have become unconscious because we have formed a new habit. So it is that acts of devotion—however brief—constantly and punctually performed, become in time the very temper of our lives, and we breathe out prayers as naturally as we breathe in the air around us.

When people plead for what they call "spontaneity" in prayer, on "praying when you feel like it," they do not realize that we actually need set times for prayer in order that we learn to pray at all times. How long these set times should be depends on our temperament and our circumstances. Some people like to settle down for a long undisturbed period, when they can concentrate. Such people will get up as early as possible in order to get the uninterrupted time, even if they have to take a great deal of trouble to find a suitable place. Other people however find long periods difficult or impossible for all kinds of good reasons, but they make up for this by praying briefly several times a day, whatever they may be doing. Some people, however, question this whole business of set times and regularity. They say frankly that in their way of life it is quite impossible. But when our Lord said that we "ought always to pray and not to lose heart," he knew our difficulties. Being used to long hours of manual work, he knew the weight of physical fatigue, and yet he says to us all, "Pray always and don't lose heart!" In our ordinary daily life prayer is not impossible for anyone. But our ways of praying have to be adapted to the life we have to live, even in the midst of noise and rush and hard work. Is it after all "impossible" for anyone to reserve five minutes in the morning and five minutes at night for brief, real, unhurried prayer? Many people have begun by doing this and then have made a habit of turning to God frequently throughout the day, whenever there was any sort of breathing space. There will be times, of course, when fatigue will be so great that our minds will not work. All we can do is to turn to God humbly, offer the fatigue as our prayer, and then close the day with the prayer of Jesus, "Father, into thy hands I commit my spirit," sure that God knows, God loves, and God understands.

It does not matter in the least what method we use, so long as we find the one that comes most naturally to us and fits in most easily with the life we have to lead. It is a mistake to despise method in the life of prayer. All prayer begins with God, it is true, and it is all his gift, but it is equally true that our Lord has told us to ask and seek and knock, and whatever helps us to do this is justified if it enables us to give ourselves more fully to God—the whole object of setting aside special times for prayer is that we may be at his disposal at all times.

THE PRACTICE OF PRAYER (Cont.)

If we have not been in the habit of praying by ourselves, we may find that when we have set aside a time for it, we soon come to the end of our resources, and we wonder how on earth we are going to fill the time! The best way to begin is to follow the example of small children who begin by "saying prayers," sometimes in their own words and sometimes in simple prayers which they have been taught, which they make their own. When we feel at a loss we may find that a hymn or a psalm or a few words from the Bible may express what we want to say. Another good way is to find some prayers in a large collection which say exactly what we want to say. We may learn these by heart, or copy them into our private notebook and thus begin to make our own book of prayers. The main thing is to use them constantly till they mean more and more to us. Simone Weil, a wonderful Frenchwoman who was seeking God with all her heart, discovered that repeating aloud to herself one of George Herbert's poems, "Love bade me welcome," led her into a wonderful experience of the love of God.

Above all, we should ask to be taught how to pray the Lord's Prayer. We learn it in our childhood, yet as we grow older we see that it contains far more than we even dreamed. A small child can learn to say it with some dim comprehension of its meaning; the greatest saint can never say it perfectly. For this prayer contains all that prayer is, and should be, but it takes a lifetime to learn to *pray* it as it should be prayed.

There are a great number of ways in which this prayer can be used and expanded, for its meaning and application are inexhaustible. Meditation on each clause, in the light of the life and teaching of our Lord, will show us how much it implies, and how much it demands. Prayed very slowly and thoughtfully, there is no end to the way in which its seven clauses may become fresh prayers every day of our lives.

Vocal prayer or the saying of prayers, the use of words in prayer, is a very important part of prayer. It helps us to clarify our desires and to express them to God, and above all it makes it possible to unite with others in prayer. It is the main part of the common prayer of the church. Vocal prayer should always be part of our private prayer, and we should treasure it greatly because it unites us with others in public worship.

In our private prayers, however, there may come a time when we feel instinctively that we want to talk less and to listen more. We feel drawn to a quieter and simpler way of praying. If we are being disciplined in the observance of our set times of prayer, we may be sure that this desire to be quieter and to speak less comes from God. Growth in prayer is always in the direction of greater simplification. We shall still need to make some simple preparation for a period of prayer—a brief prayer to the Holy Spirit for his guidance, reading slowly a few verses from the Bible, or a hymn, or a prayer, in

order "to set our minds in tune." Then we can turn
wholly toward God, looking up to him, waiting upon
him, and then offering very brief prayers of praise,
adoration, or thanksgiving. Possibly we shall find it best
to repeat each phrase or "act of prayer" several times
over till its essence has been absorbed. Between each
brief act there should be a pause of silence. Gradually,
after a time, we may find that our words become fewer
and the silences longer and longer. We may even begin
to wonder whether we are praying at all. There are
two signs which will show us whether we are praying
in the way God means us to do. The first is when all
our silent prayer is summed up in a heartfelt and determined act of self-offering. This shows that God is drawing us to himself through the silence and dimness and
even the darkness. The second point is this: if the effect
of this simple prayer is to leave us with a far stronger
determination than ever to do the will of God and to
care for nothing else at all, then we know that we are
on the right track. Sometimes we may feel rather like
the disciples on Mount Hermon when a cloud came
down and enveloped them, and they were afraid. They
could only keep still and wait for the cloud to lift, but
out of the cloud they heard the voice of God . . . and
when the cloud lifted they found they were alone with
Christ, who had been with them all the time.

However determined we may be to follow the way of
prayer, we are bound to come up against certain difficulties, which may constitute a severe temptation; they
may indeed test the reality of our faith to the uttermost.

What often happens is something like this: we feel moved—as we believe by God—to begin to pray in earnest, or to try to go further along the way of prayer. For a time all goes well. We find new zest in prayer and we feel that we are really making some progress. Then—we do not know why—the freshness wears off, we feel dull and listless and are filled with a strong disinclination for private prayer and for public worship. If we find that this listlessness is not due to fatigue or ill health, or to flat disobedience to the will of God, we may be tempted to feel that we have made a mistake and we must give it all up. This temptation must be resisted at all costs. But we may find some relief from this tension by realizing that what we are going through is a normal experience. We were never meant to live on a dead level. Oscillations are of the law of life in most spheres that touch us closely. We all know the flatness of reaction after a great joy or a great sorrow, or even after a supreme effort. We feel as though we shall never feel "alive" again. Yet our common sense tells us that this is a normal and inevitable experience which must be borne till it has worked itself out. We need times in life when we lie fallow, and live from day to day, without much thought for the future. But life goes on, and, gradually, almost unconsciously, we feel the flow of life again. Oscillations are only to be expected in the spiritual life as well as on every other level. Biologists point out that "what characterizes the living organism is its biological constants such as the composition of the blood, the temperature of warm-blooded animals . . . blood pressure. With each of these constants there is a certain margin of normal oscillation, which may be compared to the slight deviation from its course of a ship, thrust now to port and now to starboard by the action of the waves. But like an automatic pilot, correcting each deviation and bringing the ship back on its course, this organic sensitivity ensures constant regulation." [1]

This principle applies to the spiritual life too. It has its frequent oscillations; it too has its regulator. There are the normal oscillations caused by doubt and various kinds of temptation, such as difficult circumstances, our personal relationships, our attitude to our work and the people with whom we have to do, our health, and a number of other things—all these provide us with plenty of things to divert us from the straight course. Then there are the more violent oscillations caused by our own self-willed action and self-assertion, amounting to actual disobedience. These are the times when we say defiantly, "I am not fussy, but must have . . . this or that." If we are truly determined to obey God in all things we shall soon realize the cause of these more violent oscillations, and we shall come back to him and ask him to forgive us and to regulate our lives and wills afresh. Then we begin to see that this way of living is normal, that this experience of falling away and recovering is the way forward. We need to pray for greater sensitivity to the voice of God that we may keep moving in the right direction and that we may be brought back when we have diverged too far. The more we pray, the more sensitive we become. On the one hand we realize more profoundly our need, our ignorance and foolishness, and,

---

[1] Paul Tournier, *A Doctor's Casebook* (London: S.C.M. Press, 1954), p. 144.

on the other hand, the boundless goodness of the grace of God.

There is another difficulty which is closely allied to this experience of oscillation. Everyone who tries to lead a life of prayer is at times troubled and perplexed by fluctuations in feeling, which make prayer so easy and pleasant when the feelings are those of joy and peace and enjoyment, and so difficult when all feeling is absent. It is not enough to say that feelings don't matter; we have been made with sensitive feelings, and it is only right and natural that we should find delight in praising the God of all love and beauty. There are times when we experience a pure delight which is evidently the gift of God. Such experiences should be accepted with humble thankfulness and should spur us on to greater delight in doing his will.

At the same time it is not safe to depend upon our feelings. As a wise Methodist minister has remarked, "If our feelings were everything, we might as well give up church religion and anything else, and buy a cylinder of nitrous oxide. I remember the one time in my life when I had a dose of it. Then as the psalmist says, 'My mouth was filled with laughter,' and my brotherly feelings towards the dentist bending over me rivalled those of St. Francis—until the effect of the gas departed." [2]

To take our feelings too seriously only leads to all the miseries of self-centeredness. After all, it is *God* we want, not our *feeling* about him. In practice this means that of course we shall go to church and Holy Communion regularly, whatever we may be feeling at the

---

[2] A. E. Whitham, *Discipline and Culture of the Spiritual Life,* p. 229.

moment, that we will keep our times of prayer and will try to be cheerful and courteous to other people, however gloomy and gray our own feelings may be on any particular day. Sometimes these periods of difficulty may be prolonged, and we shall be afraid that we have done something wrong and that God is displeased with us. Then is the time to make acts of faith in God's goodness and love, and to try to help others in every way we can, while doing our level best to be prompt and efficient in our discharge of duty.

Some years ago I crossed the Alps twice in one day through the tunnel of St. Gotthard. It was a bright autumn day, and the sun was shining brightly as we began the ascent. Then we plunged into the darkness, up and up, and round and round we went, light and darkness following each other in swift succession. But at every turn in the ascent, as I looked out of the train window I could see that at every bend in the spiral route we were much higher up the mountainside. If we could have gone higher still we would have come out into a light so brilliant that we would have had to veil our faces for the glory of that light on the dazzling snow "The darkness and the light are both alike to thee. . . . Thou hast beset me behind and before, and laid thine hand upon me."

PRAYER AND THOUGHT

The relation between thought and prayer is very important. To some people, however, any use of the mind in prayer is regarded as a hindrance rather than a help. Others find the intellectual aspect of religion so fascinating that they pay too much attention to it, to the neglect of prayer, self-discipline, and loving service. This lack of balance, which may lead to dangerous self-deception, is due to the fact that the centrality of God, and what theologians call his "prevenience," have been ignored. Such people have either forgotten, or failed to realize that this is God's world. Not only has he created it, but "his action floods the universe." He is ever pouring out his creative power and his love and mercy upon us. His sun shines upon the evil and the good. The whole universe is impregnated with his presence, as the fragrance of lime blossom perfumes the air on a warm summer day; it is unseen, and may be scarcely noticed, but it fills the air with its sweetness. "He filleth all in all." Not only does he fill every crevice of our world, but nothing can keep him out. Yet unless we believe this, we do not realize that he is speaking to us all the time. "He is offering himself to us at every moment, in every place," says an old French writer. "When I see this . . . everything becomes bread to feed me, fire to purify me, a chisel to shape me according to the heavenly pattern. Everything becomes an instrument of grace for my necessities. Now I see that the one I used to seek in other directions is himself seeking me incessantly, and giving himself to me in everything that happens." [1] All we have to do is to receive him as he comes to us and let him do with us what he will.

So when we begin to think and pray, first of all we remind ourselves that God is seeking us, that, therefore, he has something to say to us—we must listen, not straining our ears to hear a voice in which we do not quite believe, but waiting on God in peace, opening our hearts and minds to him—letting him in.

Listening involves thought and prayer. We have to come near enough to hear, to be able to pick up the message which is addressed to us by name, with the prayer in our hearts, "Speak, Lord, for thy servant heareth." This means being willing to wait in his presence, patiently, humbly, quietly, and obediently. For just as there is a special vocation for each of us within our general vocation as Christians, so there is a special word for each of us, within the general content of God's message.

There are two ways of listening which have been found, throughout the inner history of the Christian church, to be among the ways in which God speaks to his people:

a) Reading religious books;

b) Meditation and Bible study.

Most of us however find that we need some kind of preparation before we can tune in and listen aright. It

---

[1] P. J. P. de Canssade, *L'Abandon à la Providence Divine*, Le P. H. Ramière, ed. (Paris, 1921), Vol. 1. English translation by Olive Wyon.

is a mistake to make a violent effort to acquire this habit and then to give it up in a fit of discouragement, saying, "It's no use! It's too difficult. I can't hear anything. It's no use to me!" There may be a number of reasons for this discouragement. Instead of yielding to this mood, it would be wiser to try to discover whether there is anything in our life which is out of tune with the will of God. For instance, in our personal relationships are we failing in love? Have we been slipping into slightly dishonest practices, excusing ourselves by saying, "Well, everybody does it. I don't set myself up to be a saint!" Are we always quite honest in money matters or in things which affect the community in which we live? Are we wasting other peoples' time by laziness and carelessness and forgetfulness, or by the habit of putting off? Have we slipped into untruthful ways of speaking, not telling lies exactly, but giving wrong impressions, or are we habitually too critical of other people and unkind and censorious in speech? Is there one part of our life which we divorce entirely from our relation to God and keep secretly for ourselves?

It is obvious that any sin which we know we have committed—though we may have tried to forget it—will make us soundproof against the voice of God. Repentance, confession, and any restitution which is possible are the only ways to remove this wall between us and God.

Another difficulty in meditation may be due to the fact that we are not sufficiently interested in God. Someone has said, "The truth is that men begin to find prayer a difficulty when they begin to find God a difficulty. This comes when God has ceased to interest them because other things have begun to interest them more." [2] In the parable of the sower, Jesus speaks of the seed that never came to fruition because it was finally strangled by the "lusts of other things entering in."

So in our preparation for the prayer of thought we need to pray for honesty of mind, a penitent heart, humility, a great desire for God, and for the continual enlightenment of the Holy Spirit. And we need to do this in quietness—quiet of body, quiet of mind, and quiet of heart. "Be still, and know that I am God."

"Spiritual reading," or the reading of religious books in order that we may hear God speak to us, is a different thing from the hurried or careless way in which we read books we do not consider to be very important. Here we have to read slowly, with full attention, but quietly and receptively, and without strain. It is a fact that God does speak to us when we set ourselves to listen. We may not always realize that it is he who is speaking when we pick up a book, perhaps rather casually, and find an apparently chance remark which throws a flood of light on a question which is perplexing us. We all know the experience of finding the right book at the right time, or those occasions when as we read with attention but with no special interest, suddenly a word, a phrase, a thought flashes across our mind, and we stop and hold our breath—for this word has come right home to us, this is the very word we needed. It comes as a sign of the will of God and of his presence in our lives. When we hear a word which we know to be the *truth*

---

[2] Edward Leen, *Progress Through Mental Prayer* (London: Sheed and Ward, 1941), p. 37.

and the *truth for us* at this particular moment in life, then we know that *God is speaking to us.*

What books should we read? This depends upon our tastes, our circumstances, our education, and our environment. No one can lay down rules for others; what feeds one person is no good to another. Religious books which make us think, which deal with the central matters of the Christian faith, are very important. Then, of course, we should read at least some of the "spiritual classics," for they contain the essence of Christian experience down the ages. Many people find good biographies of great Christian men and women—saints, prophetic persons, missionaries, scholars, thinkers, and reformers—more fruitful than books on doctrine, or expositions of the "spiritual life" in the abstract. Further, if we are on the alert to listen for the voice of God there is no need to restrict our reading entirely to books that are labeled "religious." God may speak to us through works on science and art, through the adventures of great travelers and explorers, through history, through poetry, and even through novels. All reading that enlarges our thought of God and of his purpose for mankind helps us to pray.

Meditation is sometimes called the prayer of thought; or mental prayer. These phrases mean the same thing: thinking about God, in order to love him. It is partly an intellectual exercise and partly a spiritual one; its aim is to lead us into prayer. It is like a springboard from which we can dive into the ocean of the love of God. That sounds simple enough. But a good many people are perplexed about it and wonder whether they could learn to do it. They tend to think that it is something abstruse, and not for ordinary people. They do not

41

realize that the actual process of meditation is something we all do, every day of our lives, sometimes with a very serious end in view, sometimes about things which may be pleasant or even trivial, but which still require some thought.

For instance, suppose you want to plan a holiday for yourself and the family. First of all there is the question, where shall we go? This raises a lot of discussion, but after a bit things become clearer as the common mind emerges and a place is chosen. Then comes the business of dates which will suit everyone, the visit to the travel agent, and perhaps some reading up about the place or country you are going to visit. Finally, the tickets are bought, the day of departure arrives, and off you go! You have made a "corporate meditation" on the subject: "Our Summer Holiday." It is a process of thought, discussion, reflection, choice, resolve, and, finally, action. A religious meditation is made on exactly the same lines, but the subject is different.

There are many methods of meditation. If one is a beginner it is wise to begin very simply. For instance, it is a good plan to choose a book in the Bible, say one of the Gospels; read slowly (after the previous preparatory prayers) and quietly, until one word or phrase or verse "hits" you. Then stop. Think about it. If possible, learn it by heart (or write it out and carry it about with you all day). Then turn the thoughts that come to you into prayer. This can be done by anyone who can read. Yet this method is often used by men and women with a long and mature Christian experience.

Another way is to take a psalm, read it very slowly and, if there is time, turn it into your own words and pray it as your own prayer. Choose one verse out of this psalm as your "word" for the day.

To some people, the imaginative reading of a story in the Gospels is a never-ending source of nourishment for their souls. (This does not apply to people whose minds are more inclined to the abstract.) Take an incident in one of the Gospels, think about it, picture it in your mind, look at our Lord in the center, note his attitude to the people round him, look at the other people in the story and note their attitude to him—look as long as you can, till you feel that you are there, on the shore of the lake, on the hills above the Sea of Galilee, on the slopes of the Mount of Olives, or in the courts of the temple in Jerusalem. It may help you to ask yourself three questions after this:

What does this story teach me about God?
What does this story teach me about myself?
What does this story teach me about God's will
    for me?

Then turn your thoughts into prayer, ending with self-offering to God. Meditation should always be related to life. A good meditation is not necessarily one in which we have been interested or even moved emotionally, but it is one which issues in acts of obedience and surrender carried out in daily life.

Here is an instance of meditation which had a very searching influence upon life. It comes from a Chinese prison. Geoffrey Bull, a young missionary to Tibet, had

43

been captured by the Chinese and was now shut up in a dark cell, alone. He says, "I had no Bible in my hand, no watch on my wrist, no pencil or paper in my pocket. There was no real hope of release. There was no real hope of life. There was no real possibility of reunion with those I loved. The only reality was my Lord and Savior Jesus Christ." [3] Yet without his Bible (which had been taken from him) he made frequent and prolonged meditations on passages of Scripture, for the Bible was not only in his well-stored mind but in his heart. Later on, after gruelling experiences of interrogation and brainwashing, he was able to write, "They had been unable to break the grip of the Hand that held me. They had been unable, in all their bitter and sustained bombardment, to dislodge God's Word within my heart." [4]

One day, when he had already been in prison for a long time and all hope of freedom seemed remote or impossible, he was reflecting upon his call to missionary service. It had been unmistakable, confirmed by many strange and inspiring experiences both outward and inward. The three years in Tibet had been exhilarating. And now he was perplexed, and he was wondering why "the opening door of Tibet" was "replaced by the closed door" of his cell. How could this be reconciled with the reality of his "call"? Then he began to think about the story of Abraham and Isaac on Mount Moriah: "In my loneliness I followed Abraham to Moriah. I watched him . . . cutting wood . . . and preparing the fire . . ."

---

[3] Bull, *op. cit.*, p. 13. (Geoffrey Bull was in prison from October 1950 to December 1953.)

[4] *Ibid.*, p. 143.

and so he went through the whole story, picturing every part of it as vividly as though he had been there.

When he had relived the story, he began to ask himself, "Can I follow the call of God as Abraham did?" And as he pondered, he asked himself what he could give that was absolutely vital to him, then and there, in that situation, at that very moment. Suddenly he saw that there was something to be surrendered which would cost him everything: "Suddenly I knew that what I called 'my call' was precisely that to me. My call had become the very life I lived. Somehow I had made it mine, when really it was always His. . . . God's call had become my career." The more he thought about this, the more he realized that even this must be given up, for what God wanted from him was not even his work in Tibet but himself, for as he says, "While I had my 'call,' in a way I had everything still, so it too must go—go back to God who gave it." Then he adds, "He still waits to know whether, with our hands unclasped, we will meet him on the hill." [5]

-----

[5] *Ibid.*, p. 98.

PRAYER AND LIFE

Here we come down to earth. Unless life and prayer are integrated, prayer becomes unreal and life unsatisfying. If the gap between the two becomes too wide, both go bad. A wonderful picture of this complete integration of prayer and life is given to us in the Gospel of St. John.

"Now . . . when Jesus knew that his hour had come to depart out of this world to the Father, having loved his own who were in the world, he loved them to the end. And during supper . . . Jesus, knowing that the Father had given all things into his hands, and that he had come from God and was going to God, rose from supper, laid aside his garments, and girded himself with a towel. Then he poured water into a basin, and began to wash the disciples' feet, and to wipe them with the towel with which he was girded."

And this was "the night in which he was betrayed," the last night he was to spend with his friends before his death. The cross was only a few hours away, and yet, at this great moment, with his heart full of sublime confidence in God, and infinite and tender love for his brethren, he took off his outer garments and knelt before each one in turn, to render a small service which they were all too proud to do for one another. He went round the circle in complete silence, only speaking in answer to Peter's impulsive expostulations. When he had done, he sat down again, and said to them, as he looked round into their faces with such gentleness and love, "Do you know what I have done to you? . . . If I then, your Lord and Teacher, have washed your feet, you also ought to wash one another's feet."

Here we see the majesty and the humility of God. He is infinitely high and holy, and yet infinitely near: "He who has seen me has seen the Father," said Jesus that same evening, possibly in the Upper Room, as they sat at table. Here life and prayer are one, in the smallest act of courtesy and service, and in the act of complete self-sacrifice. Jesus tells us plainly: this is how we ought to live, because he has given us an example of love in action which everyone can follow. From adoration we must go straight to the humblest tasks, or to the utmost limits of self-sacrifice.

So we must begin where we are. That is the first essential. We begin with *facts,* not with daydreams—the facts of our homes and families, of the place where we live, and the people we meet every day, at home, at church, in the office, or shop, or school, or factory, or anywhere else. Then there is the fact of our job. We may like it, or we may only do it because there seems to be no other way of earning a living, but it is a *fact* and must be faced. The same applies to all the circumstances of our lives. We may be happy in them, or we may dislike and resent them, but they are there—to be faced and either accepted or altered. If we believe that we are not intended to live in them for the rest of our life, through prayer we shall gain wisdom and strength to change them. If not, then complete acceptance of the situation as the will of God for the moment will bring peace and stability into our lives. The future, for the moment, must be left in God's hands. When his time comes, we may be sure that he will give us the help we need to come out of a difficult situation.

This habit of facing facts, honestly and squarely, is closely connected with the meaning of vocation. We can face facts more courageously and wisely if we are sure that the world is not ruled by chance, if we believe, as Christians, that this is God's world, that he is in control of all things, including the circumstances of our own lives. It is not childish to think that God is concerned in our affairs. He has a great and glorious purpose for the whole world, and within that purpose he has a definite part for each one of us to play. It is most important to realize that vocation applies to us all, not only to parsons, missionaries, doctors and nurses, or teachers. We are all called to obedience to God's will in all things, it is true, but the meaning of life is greatly enhanced when we realize that for each one of us there is also a special vocation. We receive this vocation from God, but not passively, as we take a letter or a telegram. No, we have to keep our minds open to events and our hearts open to God, often having to wait about and go through long periods of uncertainty, which seem like wasted time but in the end we see that they are really part of the vocation itself. Our vocation may be fulfilled in a great many different ways, both outward and inward. For some it comes in the form of positive achievement, from the creative life of the home and the family out into all kinds of public service, in education or research, in the sphere of medicine or administration, or in social reform or politics and the like; or it may come in the shape of work as an artist, writer, poet, musician, or craftsman; for others, in the thousand and one jobs in business, industry, commerce, or agriculture, on which the welfare of the community depends. In many of these vocations there is the reward of outward success, or at least the feeling that one has made a vital contribution to human welfare, whether it is recognized or not.

But there are other kinds of vocations which are much more difficult to recognize and accept: sometimes expressed in suffering and apparent failure, when often all that we can do is to be and to endure. Others have to spend their lives in uncongenial or hard and unrequited work, which yields nothing but disappointment to the person concerned though the work itself may be useful and necessary. Such experiences, even if sometimes they seem to have no pattern, and be nothing but bits and pieces, may become a real and fruitful vocation if offered to God; then what seems like frustration becomes creative and worthwhile. For with God there is no waste.

This is no mere theory; this whole view of life as vocation is based upon the deepest truth of the incarnation. All the experiences of Jesus as man, all that he learned from the years of which we know nothing in Nazareth, and all that he went through in Galilee and Jerusalem, were gathered up in his final offering on the cross and brought to fruition in his risen manhood through the resurrection. From the human point of view much of his life on earth must have seemed to have consisted of a great many unrelated odds and ends. Yet when God raised him from the dead on Easter Day, he "took these

49

bits and pieces of a disjointed ministry and wove from them a single garment of salvation for the whole world." [1] Nothing that he had done or suffered upon earth was lost or wasted. God accepted, used, and transformed it all into the perfect pattern of redemption. So we too, united with him, are also raised up complete in him and victorious over time and death, and all that seems contrary to his will. For "he must reign," and we are "partakers of his resurrection." When we realize this, when we see that each life is ennobled by the call of God and made fruitful by Christ's risen life, we are able to take each day as it comes, as a fresh gift from God. This of course includes all the circumstances in it, as part of his will for us, whatever they may be. This does not mean that he "sends" all kinds of difficulties and frustration, but that in every situation we can find and do the will of God. There may be periods in life when our time seems to be frittered away in trivial and commonplace matters, yet even in such a situation we can live in peace because we believe that for the moment this is the way appointed for us, though we do not understand it at all. We can live like this because we are sure of God and because we know that his love and power are at the helm and that he fills every part of life with meaning.

We must begin where we are. For many people the heavy responsibilities of home and family and earning a living absorb all their time and strength. Yet such a home—where love is—may be a light shining in a dark place, a silent witness to the reality and the love of God.

We must begin where we are, but once we have put

---

[1] H. A. Williams, *Jesus and the Resurrection,* p. 67.

ourselves and our lives into God's hands, to be used as he wills, and when and where, we must be on the alert, peacefully busy, but inwardly watching for signs of the will of God in the ordinary setting of our lives. To ears which have been trained to wait upon God in silence, and in the quietness of meditation and prayer, a very small incident, or a word, may prove to be a turning point in our lives, and a new opening for his love to enter our world, to create and to redeem.

Christian history is full of examples of this truth. For instance, the final abolition of slavery in the modern world was due, in its beginnings, to an unknown man, John Woolman, an American Quaker. At that time everybody kept slaves and the wealthy Quakers with the rest. John Woolman had grown up in this society and had taken slavery for granted until a day came when his employer told him to make out a bill-of-sale for a woman slave, a young woman who was a member of their household. Until that moment Woolman had not thought about the question of slavery at all. Now he felt uneasy, but he was not clear in his mind, so he did what he was told and felt very unhappy. Finally he told his employer that he believed "slave-keeping to be inconsistent with the Christian religion." For the moment that was all, but it was not the end of the matter. Woolman's mind was very concrete. When he was confronted by a fact, he thought out a theory of conduct before he dealt with it. So it was five years before he had thought out his position on slavery, and it was more than ten years before he began to speak it out in public. From that time onward until his death, he never ceased to make a vigorous attack upon the whole system of slavery. It

cost him a great deal, in time, and traveling, and un-
popularity, and suffering. Sometimes the burden seemed
almost more than he could bear for he became increas-
ingly sensitive to every kind of human misery. Then
he turned to prayer, and found strength to go on to the
end.[2]

Elizabeth Fry was led into her great work for prisoners
by being asked to make baby clothes for the naked
babies in Newgate Prison. So quietly and almost casually
did her vocation unfold—it came through a call from
without for a practical service which any woman could
give. When she went to Newgate with a bundle of
little garments she had no idea that, at that moment, for
her the hour of destiny had struck.[3]

The Abbé Pierre, speaking in Paris in 1955, tells us
how his great work for suffering and homeless people
began: "When I started, in the humblest, obscurest way,
by helping a human being in my street who was sleeping
in the open, this began to arouse the public conscience.
It began to awaken it to the sort of feeling for humanity
that we've got to awaken on a world scale." [4]

Again, it was the sight of a child dying of starvation
in the Sicilian village of Trappeto that turned Danilo
Dolci, a young architect, into one "of the most pas-
sionate reformers of our time." Dissatisfied with his
successful life in the north of Italy he went south to this
miserable village because he had heard that it was a
place of terrible poverty and misery. When he reached
Trappeto, he found men living like animals, people turn-

_____

[2] Janet Whitney, *John Woolman, Quaker* (London: Harrap, 1943).
[3] Janet Whitney, *Elizabeth Fry* (London: Harrap, 1937), pp. 142ff.
[4] Pierre, *op. cit.*, p. 78.

ing to crime simply to get food for their starving children, wives and families left to starve when their husbands were caught and sent to prison. He was appalled by this distress and decided, then and there, to give his whole life to helping them. Now and then he has fasted for long periods in order to draw the attention of the government to this distress. He is often called the "Gandhi of Sicily." He is not a politician. His main work until now has been to establish centers for research in full employment, free dispensaries and clinics, and adult education centers. He has married the widow of a fisherman with five children. They have four children of their own and have adopted four more. Aldous Huxley describes Dolci as the "ideal twentieth century saint." [5]

We must begin where we are, but we must not stay there. But we must begin by "being" rather than by "doing." That is, we must have love in our hearts before we can give love to others. *We* cannot generate love simply by wishing it; what we need is the love of Christ taking hold of us and pouring out to others, to those nearest to us, where we so often fail, to the people we meet casually, in various ways—so often we ignore them as persons and only think of them in relation to our comfort or convenience—and then in an ever widening circle to all whom we can help in any way by love and prayer. This may sound easy, but often we shall find it is very hard, especially if we meet with coldness or an icy reserve which erects an apparently insuperable barrier.

[5] *The London Sunday Times,* March 29, 1959.

Such an experience is testing. It may tempt us to withdraw into proud isolation, or to feel impatient and to say inwardly, "It's no good! I give up! I wash my hands of him or her!" Nothing but living in the love of God for ourselves, and knowing his forbearance and patience with us, will enable us to hold on in the will to love. Day by day our one aim must be to try to put love and humility first in our prayers and our desires, to be resolved never to let indifference or impatience or irritation or evasion take the place of the will to love, keeping our hearts open to the love of God who loves us to the end, and to the uttermost, and will never let us go.

We must begin where we are, but we must be ready to go further. It is not enough to be ready to answer a call for help when it forces itself upon our attention. As Christians we are called to love the whole world—the world for which Christ died—the whole human family. For all over the world there is not only the problem of physical hunger and the threat of famine, there is a famine of love, a famine of the spirit. When Geoffrey Bull was in a Chinese prison, exposed to continual assaults upon his mind and his whole personality, the most terrible thing to him was not merely the experience of brainwashing, but the fact that he was living and suffering in a world without love. We all know that little children in institutions may die for lack of love, however carefully and scientifically they are handled. All over the world men and women and children are famishing for love, to be understood, to be welcomed, to be loved. Physical suffering is bad enough, but mental and spiritual suffering work still more havoc in the human spirit.

So as Christians we are called to open our hearts to the whole world, to face the facts of human suffering and distress. Hunger, sickness, and disease, crime and prisons, bad housing and loveless homes are all facts of which we are more or less aware. They should confront each of us with a personal challenge, making us ask ourselves, What can *I* do about this?

In that searching parable of the last judgment when the whole of mankind stands before the Son of man on the throne of his glory, there is no distinction of persons, and there is only one test: *love.*

For some of us the challenge of this story arouses us to a new sense of urgency in obedience to the call of love. Others feel the burden of human misery so intensely that they are almost overwhelmed by it. They are sometimes tempted to give it all up, because, as they say, "nothing we do will be of any use! It isn't worthwhile!" If we ever feel like this we would do well to read the Gospels once more and notice how much time Jesus gave to individuals in need, and then listen to his own words about the value of a cup of cold water given in his name. Once more we see we must begin with God; all our efforts to help others must be inspired and sustained by his love, and by the knowledge that the smallest act of service or sacrifice is known and treasured by him as done unto himself. Life and prayer become integrated when prayer issues in service, and when service drives us to prayer. For in prayer we gain a new insight into our calling as Christians and a new power to fulfil it. It is a great help to realize that when we go to prayer we are not alone, we are part of the whole church universal, the "royal priesthood." In a still deeper way, we are not alone in our prayer. When we feel empty and cold and lacking in love, we can step, as it were, in a moment, "into the holiest," joining our imperfect, inarticulate, burdened prayers with the unceasing prayer of Christ, our great High Priest. For it is not *our* love and *our* efforts which will change men's hearts, but only the all-powerful love of Jesus. Praying in this way means that we can offer not only our good desires, our fervent prayers, but our prayers of confession and penitence, our prayers of acceptance, offering up as hidden sacrifices all the painful, uncongenial elements in our lives, even our failures—we can lay them all on the altar. Nothing is too great and nothing is too small for Christ to use. In the words of Lilias Trotter: "Christ's intercession is not a massing of generalities. His heart is large enough to go into the little details of our lives. It is these that he kindles with burning coals of fire from the altar. And through all these little things the great glow of his great love streams out." [6]

---

[6] Padwick, *op. cii.*, p. 180.

THE AIM OF PRAYER

The first cause of all prayer and worship, as we have seen, is the fact of God, the One Reality—half-realized by those who are "feeling after" him, accepted with adoring delight by those who have been "found" by him. "Worship," says Evelyn Underhill, "always means God, and the priority of God." Nowhere does this come out more clearly than in the Lord's Prayer which is a complete instruction in prayer. Here the glory of God comes first, the needs of man second. Yet all are included in the one overarching reality of God, the living One, who is eternal Love. These seven clauses cover every aspect of prayer, both corporate and personal, private and public. It is the prayer of the whole church, praying *for,* and *with,* the whole family of mankind.

As we enter into the meaning of this prayer, we begin to see that the aim of prayer is not primarily the comforting or enrichment of the person praying, but the transformation of the whole of life to the glory of God. Thus the aim of worship is both creative and redemptive. And the very order of the Lord's Prayer is significant— God and his glory, then man and his needs, thus reversing our inveterate tendency to put ourselves, our needs and desires first, and everything else second.

So adoration is the first and fundamental movement in all prayer, whether we are worshiping with others

57

in a great cathedral, or alone in the silence of our own
room, or in the quietness of the hills. First of all, Jesus
teaches us to look up and say, "Our Father, who art in
heaven, hallowed be thy name." We may not always find
it easy to do this, but we can try. When we are in an
Alpine valley we lift up our eyes unto the hills and gaze
and gaze. Sometimes there is nothing to see, the hills
are hidden under a veil of cloud and mist. But we do
not conclude that they have disappeared for good! We
know that they are *there;* then the clouds lift and the
hills shine out again, blue and lovely against the clear
sky. At other times they are half-veiled in mist, but in
between there are glimpses of brilliant sunlight, and on
showery days there are broken rainbows, suggesting
depths of distance and beauty out of sight. It is the
same with our experiences of worship. Sometimes we
are able to kneel in awe and adoration, with hearts which
are entranced by the beauty which we dimly see, and
still more by the conviction that here is the goal of our
heart's desire: "Thou dost excite us to delight in praising
thee." At other times we have no impulse to pray; we
feel we ought to do so, perhaps, but we feel quite blank.
Then is the time to turn resolutely away from our feelings, or our lack of them, and praise God for what he is,
eternally *there.* Such prayer is true adoration, for here
we forget ourselves and look up only to God; we are
sure of him, whether we are in darkness or in light. So
we give thanks for his great glory. We give thanks
that he is God, "only and divinely like himself." We
praise him because he is love eternal, and because we
know that the whole future of the universe is in his

hands. "All is well, and all shall be well. Glory be to God for all things!"

But there are times when we are weighed down by our own troubles and perplexities, or still more, by the needs and troubles of others. We then feel as though we cannot praise God, and sometimes we do not even try to do so. Then is the moment to make a resolute effort to turn away from ourselves, and all that is oppressing our minds and hearts, perhaps with the brief prayer of the psalmist: "My soul cleaveth unto the dust, quicken thou me, according to thy word." When we are in this mood, it is a good thing to turn our thoughts to the beauty and goodness in the world around us, and then, by the ladder of thanksgiving, gradually to rise from the simplest things that move our hearts to thankfulness, to that point where we realize that God is pure joy, the ocean and source of all joy, and the giver of joy to all his children.

The essence of the prayer of adoration, however, is always the attitude and act of self-offering. This offering of ourselves is the most real and the most effective prayer that we can ever offer. For in it we hand ourselves over to God to be taught, guided, disciplined, and used for his purpose, and for that alone. Such prayer may be expressed in words it is true, but in its essence it is beyond word, beyond thought, and beyond feeling. It is the heart of our whole being surrendered to God, without conditions.

In the second part of the Lord's Prayer we turn from the glory of God to the actualities of our human situation, to our limitations, perplexities, burdens, and sinful-ness. Yet, when we pause to think, we may realize with a shock of surprise the deep tenderness and understand-ing that lies behind this teaching of our Lord. He tells us to pray for these things because he knows us, and he knows how we feel. He knows our need and he has compassion upon us for he knows what it is to be human. No human need, he suggests, is ever alien to the thought and care of God, our heavenly Father. So adora-tion leads to the prayer of petition, when we turn from offering to asking—asking for the most fundamental human necessities, for food and forgiveness, guidance, and protection.

Here we see the paradox of Christian prayer: the summons to adore the infinite perfection of God, to sur-render to his will, to live only that his kingdom may come; and, then, the admission of our absolute de-pendence. As we pray these final clauses, we admit, quite literally, that we cannot live without him. We depend upon him for every need of body, mind, and spirit. We need more than food, we need forgiveness and we need his generous encouragement to get up and go on again after repeated falls. For many people, the sense of sinfulness comes late in the life of prayer. Still later do we come to feel our helplessness. Only then do most of us begin to see how vulnerable we are, how weak and inconstant, how ignorant and often mistaken in our choices and judgments, in a word, how much we *need* his help, guidance, and protection. It is usually the most mature Christian who prays most truly, "Hold up my goings in thy paths, that my footsteps slip not."

And as we pray this prayer for ourselves, we come

to have a greater understanding of others' temptations, and we pray *with* them, that "we" may be forgiven, delivered from evil, and kept in the right way. Seen in this light, we know that the prayer of petition is never a self-centered asking for a private need. Rather is it a childlike, trustful prayer, based on the certainty of our Father's love and wisdom. Its aim is that we may be forgiven, supported, guided, and rescued from evil, not for our own sakes, but in order that we may be able to know and do his will, and thus be used for the fulfilment of his purpose. Prayer of this kind is always answered.

So the prayer of petition "in Christ's name" widens out into intercession. In one sense, the whole of the Lord's Prayer is intercession. It begins with *Our* Father, and prays for *us* all through.

The heart of intercession, as of adoration, is offering— the offering of ourselves to God for him to use, in his way, and for his ends. That is why intercession is so closely allied with adoration. Many of the difficulties connected with the prayer of intercession would disappear if we realize this more fully. We must always begin with worship; this is indispensable and fundamental. If we fail to do this and rush into intercession full of our own ideas and think only of the human side of prayer, we shall often get bogged down, due to the fact that we are regarding intercession as a purely self-induced effort.

When we find intercession difficult we may also remind ourselves that prayer is closely connected with the intention which controls our life as a whole. Now much of our life can only gradually be brought under God's control. This takes place through what the Bible calls "dying to self," in order that we may "live unto God." This is a prolonged process. We have to accept a good deal of discipline, if we are to become more supple and obedient. So we must not be discouraged if we find that we cannot pray as we would like to do. It takes time and patience to let God have his way with us, and while this is going on we shall often be painfully aware of conflict within. But God loves us, and he is very patient, and we shall become more obedient and humble as time goes on, and our prayer will become more "of a piece" with our whole life, as the unification of our desires and impulses is accomplished by the grace of God.

Intercession is expressed in many different ways, by detailed prayer for specific ends, causes, and persons, or by momentary remembrance in the midst of a busy life, or by deep and prolonged prayer for some specific end which seems to be "laid upon the heart" as a burden of love. Then there are times when intercessory prayer does not seem to have any definite purpose in view, it is simply "poured out, an offering of love," in order that it may be used. "This," says Evelyn Underhill, "is specially true of its more developed forms in the interior life of devoted souls." Such offerings are made in silence and secrecy, known to God alone. But those who pray in this way have a deep conviction that as the result of their prayer something *happens* in the world of spirit. This prayer is sacrificial, and is a permanent element in the life of prayer in the whole church, all down the

62

centuries. Intercession of this kind greatly extends the range of our prayer. It was of such prayer that Cardinal Mercier was thinking when he wrote in a pastoral letter to his flock: "Through an ever closer adherence to the Holy Spirit in the sanctuary of your soul, you can, from within your home-circle, the heart of your country, the boundary of your parish, overpass all earthly frontiers, and intensify and extend the kingdom of love."

Intercession which is as wide as the world and as spacious as the purpose of God, springs out of a heart that is surrendered to the love of God; it finds expression both in prayer, and in action, as *identification*—identification with God in Christ, and with the whole family of mankind. This longing for identification is more widespread than we sometimes realize. When we try to intercede, in the largest and deepest way possible, it is an inspiration to know that we are joining in prayer not only with our fellow-Christians, but with many people outside the visible church. We may think of Antoine de Saint-Exupéry, for instance, the French writer, poet, airman, scientist, and inventor. He was filled with this thirst for identification with other persons. Now and again he had experiences of fusion with others—for instance, when he was in a group of men, perhaps formerly complete strangers—which filled him with joy. He also found this "unity" with others in "a sacrifice freely accepted for the common good."

It was this thirst for identification which impelled the modest, retiring Abbé Couturier, in middle life, to go out into the world as an Apostle of Unity. He had a deep sense of unity "with all saints" and "with all men." When he prayed, he strove to carry all the world in his heart. In a way so typical of him, he used to say:

"To pray unites us with the cosmos.

"To pray unites us with God, the Holy Trinity.

"To pray unites us with God's act of creation." [1]

So prayer is like an ever-flowing spring, recreating human life at its center. "Prayer," says P. T. Forsyth, "opens a fountain perpetual and luminous at the center of our personality, where we are sustained because we are created anew and not merely refreshed. For here the springs of life continually rise." [2] It must be so, for God is the eternal fountain, and as we drink of his living water, it springs up within us "to everlasting life."

The nature of Christian prayer is summed up in these impressive words of P. T. Forsyth: "We are taught [in the New Testament] that we seek only because he has found, we beseech him because he first besought us. The prayer that reached heaven began there when Christ went forth. . . . Our prayer is the answer to God's. Herein is prayer, not that we prayed him, but that he first prayed us, in giving his Son to be a propitiation for us. The heart of the atonement is prayer—Christ's great self-offering to God in the Eternal Spirit. . . . Any final glory of human success or destiny rises from man being God's continual creation and destined by him for him. So we pray because we were made for prayer, and God draws us out by breathing himself in." [3] Or, in the words of George Herbert, "Prayer is . . . God's breath in man returning to its birth."

---

[1] M. Villain, *L'Abbé Paul Couturier*, p. 300.

[2] P. T. Forsyth, *The Soul of Prayer*, p. 47.

[3] *Ibid.*, pp. 14-15.

HOW TO BEGIN

A Suggested Form of Prayer

for Daily Use

The aim of this form of prayer is to provide a framework of vocal prayer for daily use, morning and evening. Each set of brief prayers should occupy about five minutes of *quiet unhurried prayer*. The form should be composed or selected by oneself, so that one is using words which *mean* something and which will come to mean more with constant use. They should be such that they can be used when we are feeling fresh in mind, and also when we are tired and disinclined for any mental effort. Therefore the words chosen should express what one knows are the deepest and most lasting desires of one's heart. Each brief prayer should be such that it suggests much more than it says. Once the habit has been formed the very words will become so familiar that no book will be needed. It would then be wise to continue to use this form as long as it remains full of meaning. When it becomes too familiar, a fresh form, and even order, might be chosen. The words should be repeated (even if in a very low voice) very slowly and reverently with a brief pause between each clause.

In the prayers which follow I am merely giving an example of the kind of thing I mean. I would only add that this method has been evolved out of experience to help people with very busy lives and very little privacy and it has proved of great value to many. It is one way of deliverance from one sense of rush; it is possible for everyone to set aside ten minutes in the day for this exercise. Some people add five minutes in the middle of the day.

MORNING
Preparation

Thou hast beset me behind and before, and laid thine hand upon me. . . . When I awake, I am still with thee.

Worship

Bless the Lord, O my soul. O Lord my God, thou art very great; thou art clothed with honor and majesty. All love, all glory, be to thee.

Dedication of the Day

Almighty God, my Father and my Savior: I offer thee my whole self for thy use this day. I offer thee my work; my thought and reading; my contacts with other people; my rest and my recreation; my joys and my sorrows; my sufferings and temptations. Do thy will in me all the day long.

Direct, control, suggest, this day,
All I design, or do, or say,
That all my powers, with all their might,
In thy sole glory may unite.

Intercession

O God, the giver of all love, I thank thee for my family and my friends. Today I pray to thee especially for——.

By thy prevailing Presence I appeal:
O fold them closer to thy mercy's breast;
O do thine utmost for their souls' true weal.

An Act of Faith

I believe in God the Father Almighty,
Maker of heaven and earth;
and in Jesus Christ his only Son, Our Lord;
And in the presence and power of the Holy Spirit,
Within me and all the children of God.

The Lord's Prayer

Our Father, who art in heaven, hallowed be thy name.
Thy kingdom come, thy will be done on earth as it is
in heaven.

Give us this day our daily bread and forgive us our
trespasses as we forgive those who trespass against us.

And lead us not into temptation, but deliver us from
evil, for thine is the kingdom, and the power, and the
glory for ever and ever.

EVENING

Preparation

Like as a father pitieth his children, so the Lord
pitieth them that fear him. For he knoweth our frame;
he remembereth that we are dust. The Lord is merciful
and gracious. From everlasting to everlasting, he is God.

Worship

Now unto the King eternal, immortal, invisible, the
only wise God, be honor and glory, for ever and ever.

Amen.

Gratitude and Penitence

Glory to thee, my God, this night,
For all the blessings of the light . . . .

Prayer

Forgive me, Lord, for thy dear Son,
The ill that I this day have done,
That with the world, myself, and thee,
I, ere I sleep, at peace may be.

Intercession

Father of mercies, God of all comfort:
I commit to thee this night:
All whom I love, especially——.
Those who suffer——
All in special need——

Lighten our darkness, we beseech thee, O Lord, and by thy great mercy defend us from all the perils and dangers of this night; for the love of thy only Son, our Savior, Jesus Christ. Amen.

Dedication of the Night

Father, I offer to thee the hours of this night: sleep, memories, thoughts, desires, and dreams.
Take all under thy control.
Father, into thy hands I commend my spirit.
Hide me under the shadow of thy wings.

An Act of Faith

I am persuaded, that neither death, nor life, nor angels, nor principalities, nor powers, nor things present, nor things to come, nor height, nor depth, nor any other creature, shall be able to separate us from the love of God, which is in Christ Jesus our Lord.

The Lord's Prayer

May the God of peace be with us all. Amen.